Jesus Is With Us Always
The Story of the Eucharist

Written and Illustrated by Eileen Cunis
Copyright © 2016 Eileen Cunis

*To My Mother
Mary Carhart*

In the beginning, God made the universe. He created the heavens and the earth, all that is seen and all that cannot be seen. Last of all, he made human beings, man and woman. Everything God made was good, and the earth was a place of peace.

The first people were named Adam and Eve. God planted a garden in Eden, and there he put the man and woman he had formed. In the cool of the day, God would walk in the garden and talk with Adam and Eve.

God said, "Of every tree of the garden, you may freely eat, but of the tree of the knowledge of good and evil, you may not eat. In the day that you eat it, you will surely die."

Now of all the good things God had made, there was a bright shining angel, who chose to turn against God. Satan hated all of God's creation, especially man and woman. So making himself to look like a serpent, he spoke to Eve, making her hungry for the forbidden fruit. She took the fruit and gave it to Adam, both of them eating and disobeying God.

The peace of the garden and of the earth was destroyed, and although Adam and Eve did not die on that day, God sent them away from Eden and from His presence. From that time, all people would have sadness. The way back to God became hard, and very few would meet Him face to face. But God gave Adam and Eve a promise: he would one day walk among people again.

Adam and Eve's family grew into many families and tribes, enough to fill towns and cities. God called a man named Abraham to lead his wife Sarah, their relatives, and servants to a new land that would be their own. Sarah and Abraham were given a baby boy, named Isaac. The Lord promised that Isaac's family would grow to be too large to count and would be known as God's own people. Through this family, God would again become a friend and father to everyone on earth.

One day, when Isaac was a boy, God told Abraham to sacrifice his son, to put him to death, as a gift to the Lord. Though he was full of sadness, Abraham began to do what the Lord had asked. He would give God what was most precious to him. But God sent an angel to stop Abraham from killing his son. Instead of Isaac, God sent a lamb for Abraham to sacrifice. The lamb that died in Isaac's place was a sign of God's own Son whom God would someday send to earth to die that all people might be saved.

Over many years, Abraham's family grew to be a great nation. They were called the people of Israel. The great Pharaoh, King of Egypt, made them his slaves and was cruel to them. When they cried out to God for help, God sent an Israelite named Moses to tell Pharaoh, "Let my people go!"

Pharaoh would not free the slaves. And so the Lord sent an angel to pass through all of Egypt, putting to death the oldest child of each family. Israel's children, though, would live, for God showed Moses how to save them. Each family was to brush the blood of a lamb around its doorway. The families stayed in their homes as the angel of death came through Egypt. Seeing the blood on the doorways, the angel passed over the homes of Israel, and their children did not die. But because of the awful deaths in the Egyptian's homes, the Pharaoh knew he must set all of Israel free.

Now the people of Israel began a long journey through the desert to their new land. God showed them the way. He gave them a bread called manna to eat and water to drink, for the desert was hot and dry and empty. Israel would always remember how the Lord set them free from slavery and cared for them on their journey. They would teach their children about the bread from heaven that gave them life in the wilderness.

One day in their travels, the people stopped to rest at a mountain called Sinai. Moses climbed up the mountain to meet with God, who gave Moses two tablets of stone. On them were written the laws called the Ten Commandments. They taught how the people should live together and how they must pray and worship God. Hearing them, everyone knew that God was good and wise, because his laws were good.

And so God brought His people to their own land. He kept teaching them and helping them. Even when they did not obey him, they knew he had chosen them for a special reason. Still, he did not speak with them as friend to friend, as he had in the garden with Adam and Eve. He would visit Israel now and then, but did not come to stay.

A long time passed, and God saw that the world was ready for His footsteps again. He sent the angel Gabriel to an Israelite home in the town of Nazareth to bring a message to Mary. God had chosen her, a young woman who was going to be married, to be the mother of His Son. When Gabriel found her, he called out, "Hail, full of grace! The Lord is with you!"

Mary wondered what this greeting meant. Gabriel said, "The Holy Spirit will come to you, and create a new child within you. This baby will be the Son of the Most High God, and you will call Him Jesus."

Trusting in God with all her heart, Mary was glad to receive His Son within her. And so God Himself came to be a tiny child, born to the people of Israel on the earth, to walk with them and meet them face to face.

Mary and Joseph married each other. Soon they went on a journey to the town of Bethlehem to pay their taxes, as the king had commanded everyone in the land. Jesus was born there, in a stable where Mary and Joseph found shelter, for there was no room for them in the inn.

That night, angels filled the skies from east to west, singing and praising God. He had come to his people! God would live with them again! But no one saw or heard the angels, except for the shepherds whose eyes and ears God had opened. And they, too, rejoiced.

When Jesus was grown, he went into the world to tell his people of God's love for them. John the Baptist was at the Jordan River, calling all of Israel to obey the commandments of the Lord. He baptized all those who were sorry for the wrong they had done and were ready to follow God. Jesus came to be baptized, too. He, the Son of God, came to take upon himself all of the blame for the sins of everyone. John said, "Behold, the Lamb of God, who takes away the sin of the world!"

Jesus walked from town to town, teaching everyone about God. He told how God the Father forgives the sins of those who are truly sorry. He blessed the children brought by their parents. Sick people who came to him were healed. Blind men were given their sight, and some who had died were even brought back to life. These miracles showed that Jesus was truly God's Son.

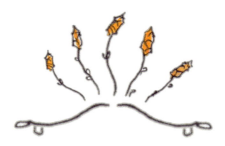

One day, many people came to hear Jesus teach. As evening came, everyone was hungry, but did not want to leave Jesus to find food. A young boy gave Jesus five small loaves of bread and two little fish, and Jesus prayed that God would bless this humble offering. He handed out the food to thousands of people, and everyone ate and was full. They were amazed, saying, "We should make Jesus our King!"

But Jesus knew that even if he were to become king, and feed people bread every day, they would not be truly happy. They would never become true friends of God, and never be free from their sins. People will not be happy until Jesus, the Son of God, lives in their hearts. And so, Jesus told them, "I am the Bread of Life." God's plan was to give all people a living bread, Jesus himself, so that they might live in heaven forever.

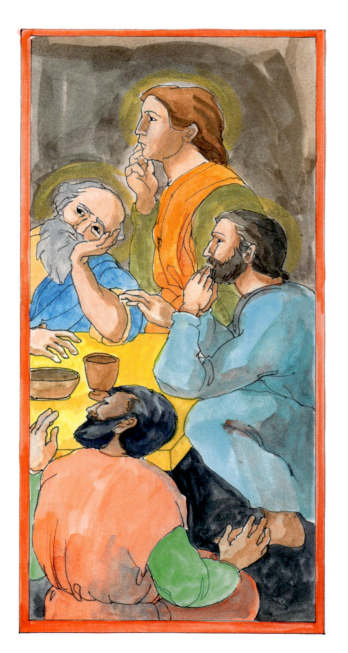

It was time for all of Israel to celebrate the Passover, remembering how God brought their people out of slavery in Egypt. Jesus gathered his closest friends, the disciples, in a quiet room to share the feast. He took bread, broke it in pieces and said, "Take this and eat it. This is my body, which will be given up for you."

Then he took the cup of wine and said, "This is the cup of my blood, poured out for many for the forgiveness of sins. Do this in memory of me."

The bread and wine, though they looked and felt, tasted and smelled the same as before, became his own Body and Blood, his own life which he shared with his friends. This meal was the first Holy Eucharist. In eating and drinking them, the disciples became part of Christ's own body. They learned a new promise: Jesus, the Son of God, would always be with them in the Eucharist.

Though Jesus had friends and disciples who loved him and believed in him, there were many who did not see that he was the Son of God. They thought that his miracles were tricks and that his teachings were dangerous lies. They wanted him to die.

Jesus was taken by soldiers and beaten badly. As the people made fun of him, he carried a heavy cross through the streets of Jerusalem. On the hill of Golgotha, Jesus was nailed to the cross. Everyone saw his pain and sorrow. As dark clouds covered the sun, and the earth shook in anger, Jesus died. It was the day we call Good Friday.

In dying, Jesus became like the lamb given to Abraham and like the lambs whose blood saved the Israelites. Jesus gave his own life so that all people would be free of sin and death. People could now be as close to God as Adam and Eve had once been – and even closer, because now they could share in his very Body and Blood. This is why he is called the Lamb of God.

The next day was Saturday. Jesus' friends were full of sorrow. They thought they would never see him again. But on Sunday morning, some of the women went to the place where his body was laid. It was gone! An angel told them, "He is risen!"

As they walked away, Jesus came to them. The women were full of wonder and joy to see that he was alive. Death could not hold God's only Son. His love and power are greater than death itself.

For forty days, Jesus appeared to his friends and followers many times. He told his disciples that the Holy Spirit would come to them, giving them power to share his life with all the world. Then, when the right time had come, Jesus was lifted up to the sky, surrounded by a cloud, and his friends could see him no longer. He returned to Heaven, to watch over and care for all the universe with God the Father. But he did not disappear. He remained with those who believe in him in the Eucharist.

 After Jesus returned to heaven, he sent the Holy Spirit to his followers. They were gathered together to pray, and suddenly a loud roaring of wind rushed around them, and it seemed as if flames of fire came upon them. The Spirit entered their hearts, and they became the Church, all of them together sharing the life of God. The Holy Spirit made them able to preach the truth of Jesus, to bring healing to the sick and forgiveness to sinners, to live together in love and peace, and to bring Jesus to the world in the Eucharist.

In these first years of Christianity, disciples of Jesus celebrated the Eucharist in each other's homes. Their celebration was much like our Mass today. As it is today, the Eucharist was their source of faith and strength. If a Christian were sick or in prison, the Eucharist would be brought to him. In times and places when it was against the law to be a Christian, Mass was held in secret. Brave believers would risk being arrested and even killed, like young St. Tarcisius, to bring Christ's Body to others.

Ever since those days, the Church has celebrated the Eucharist with great joy and thanksgiving. All of the saints have loved the Eucharist and depended upon it to be able to live the way Jesus taught us. Some saints are known especially for their love of the Body and Blood of Christ.

    The Holy Spirit comes to Mass today. He enters the bread and wine on the altar, and changes them into the Body and Blood of Christ. The people share and eat this Holy Communion, just as the disciples did at the Last Supper. In the Eucharist, the Holy Spirit brings Jesus to be with us always.

    All over the whole world, believers go to Mass every day. At every moment, someone somewhere is sharing Jesus in the Eucharist. He is living all over the earth, and will keep coming to us until the end of time. The Eucharist is the greatest way that God gives himself to people.

    The Eucharist is always being celebrated in heaven. The Lamb of God, Jesus, is on a throne in the midst of angels and saints who sing songs without end. They thank Jesus for coming to earth as a man, to die as a sacrifice for every person. They praise him for rising from the dead, and for sending the Holy Spirit to earth. When we come to Mass and worship Jesus, we join all of these people of heaven. They are singing with us!

    The Sacred Host and Precious Blood we are given at Holy Communion do not look like Jesus. God comes in a mysterious way, and many do not see him. We must believe with the faith God gives us that God is truly with us in the Eucharist. He comes as he came to Adam and Eve in the Garden. He looks for hearts that are ready for his love, and he enters them.

Scripture References

Pp. 3-5	Genesis 1:1 – 2:22, the story of creation and the fall of man.
Pp. 6-7	Genesis 12:1-9; 15:1-21, 21:1-7, the call of Abraham and birth of Isaac; Genesis 22:1-19, the sacrifice of Isaac.
Pp. 8-9	Exodus 1:8-14; chs. 7-12, Moses, Passover and Exodus.
Pp. 10-11	Exodus 19, 20:1-20, also 24; God gives Moses the law.
Pp. 12-13	Luke 1:26-38, the Annunciation.
Pp. 14-15	Luke 2:1-20, the Nativity.
P. 16-17	John 1:19-34, the Baptism of Christ; general Gospels about Jesus' life.
P. 18-19	John 6, the feeding of the 5,000.
Pp. 20-21	Matthew 26:17-29, also Mark 14:12-25 and Luke 22:7-23, the Last Supper.
Pp. 22-23	Matthew 27, also Mark 15 and Luke 23, the Crucifixion.
P. 24	Matthew 28 version of the Resurrection.
P. 25	Matthew 28:16-20 version of the Ascension, also Acts 1.
P. 26	Acts 2:1-4, Pentecost
Pp. 30-31	The vision of Heaven: Revelations chs. 4 and 5.

There are many wonderful adult books about the Eucharist. Especially recommended is *God Is Near Us*, by Joseph Cardinal Ratzinger (Holy Father Benedict XVI). For its beauty and wisdom, please read John Paul II's encyclical *Ecclesia de Eucharistia*, from which the following passage is taken:

I have been able to celebrate Holy Mass in chapels built along mountain paths, on lakeshores and seacoasts; I have celebrated it on altars built in stadiums and in city squares… This varied scenario of celebrations of the Eucharist has given me a powerful experience of its universal and, so to speak, cosmic character. Yes, cosmic! Because even when it is celebrated on the humble altar of a country church, the Eucharist is always in some way celebrated on the altar of the world. It unites heaven and earth. It embraces and permeates all creation. The Son of God became man in order to restore all creation, in one supreme act of praise to the One who made it from nothing. He, the Eternal High priest who by the blood of his cross entered the eternal sanctuary, thus gives back to the Creator and Father all creation redeemed. He does so through the priestly ministry of the Church, to the glory of the Most Holy Trinity. Truly this is the mysterium fidei which is accomplished in the Eucharist: the world which came forth from the hands of God the Creator now returns to him redeemed by Christ (EdE 8).

Made in the USA
Columbia, SC
28 September 2019